A 30-DAY DEVOTIONAL

JUNIOR

MAKING SENSE OF IT ALL

LARS ROOD

YouthMinistry.com/TOGETHER

Junior
Making Sense of It All

© 2013 Lars Rood

group.com
simplyyouthministry.com

Credits
Author: Lars Rood
Executive Developer: Nadim Najm
Chief Creative Officer: Joani Schultz
Editor: Rob Cunningham
Cover Art and Production: Veronica Preston

ISBN   978-0-7644-9004-0

10 9 8 7 6 5 4 3 2 1   20 19 18 17 16 15 14 13

Printed in the U.S.A.

TO KAIJE:

One of these days you will be a junior. You're the kind of kid who is always wanting to figure things out and to learn more about things. You're a reader like me. Kaije, I love you, and this book makes me think of you.

CONTENTS

INTRODUCTION

If you've read the previous books in this series, you know that we've focused on growing in your faith and figuring out what maturity looks like. It's now time to start piecing it all together and seeing who you are and what that means for you. All of life is a process, and you don't have to have it all figured out right now. But this is the year when you have to start figuring out a lot of things.

Figuring out who you are doesn't mean who you are *going* to be, but simply who you are right now. This is a starting point as you begin doing a lot of self-evaluation. We're more focused on the past than on the future. Who are you right now? What do you believe? What do you care about? How do you look at the world? This is the year that a lot of those questions need to get answered.

Are today's answers the final ones you'll give in your life? Not likely. Your answers and your beliefs about things may change in the coming years, but you do need to figure out some of what you believe right now because you are on the cusp of making some major decisions about the future and charting your life's direction. You will need to base a lot of those decisions upon how you are experiencing and living life right now.

How this book works:

This devotional includes 30 short things for you to think about. For each reading you'll find some sort of story and some follow-up questions to consider. You can do these by yourself, but you also can benefit from discussing them with a small group of people. This book might become 30 weeks of curriculum or simply provide 30 days of focus before the school year starts.

Each devotion includes a section called "The World Thinks." Most often these are comments that I have heard from non-Christians about these particular topics or issues. I don't hold back, so they may come across as a little negative. That's OK. You'll hear negative things all the time about your faith. The point is to encourage you to think through what people say and work out how you might respond to the thoughts and reactions people have about your faith in Christ.

You'll also find an action step for each devotion that is exactly what it sounds like: an opportunity to actually do something to discover and apply key truths. Often these are things that take some effort to accomplish and can help you grow. I want to encourage you to really put effort into doing them. Finally, I've included some Bible passages for you to look up—sometimes several, but often just one or two. I want you to go deeper and explore other places in the Bible with more thoughts, stories, truths, and ideas that will help you.

It's my hope and prayer that these devotions will challenge you, encourage you, and put you in places where you will have the opportunity to make sense of it all.

SECTION 1

DO YOU KNOW WHO YOU ARE?

547 548 549

My junior year of high school was the year I finally felt like I knew who I was. I hadn't reached my full potential, but it was the year I figured out a lot of what I liked, what I was good at, and some of what I thought I wanted to spend more time focusing on. Maybe you haven't had a lot of conversations about who you are, but this is the year to do that. You have the potential to offer a lot to those around you, so it's time to step it up.

It may not feel like the world really cares right now, but I want you to know how valuable you are. If you asked a lot of adults if they knew who they were as high school juniors, they might give you some answers about things they were involved in or things they liked. But as far as defining who they were, that question would be a lot harder. I don't remember my youth pastor asking hard questions like this, but I wish he had. I would have appreciated the opportunity to explore these real issues more because I needed to be pushed to figure that out as I was dealing with some tough relational, social, and spiritual situations where knowing myself better would have helped me with some answers.

NO. 1 HOW COMFORTABLE ARE YOU WITH YOU?

I bought a lunchbox my junior year of high school. Sounds geeky, right? Well, it was—but I was OK with that. I finally decided that year that I was just going to start doing the things I liked and not worry about what everyone else thought about me. So every day I went to school with a backpack on my shoulder, a saxophone case in one hand, and a He-Man® lunchbox in the other. That's who I was—and I was comfortable with it.

Curiously, no one ever made fun of me for that choice. I sort of expected it to happen, but it didn't. It seemed that as I learned to be comfortable with myself, others became comfortable with who I was, too. I'm not telling you to go buy a superhero lunchbox, but I do encourage you to start thinking more about the things that you like and the things that define you, and to start becoming more comfortable with yourself. God has made you exactly the way he planned, and your job is to figure out how to thrive with that reality.

THINK ABOUT:

1. How comfortable are you with what you know you really like and with who you are?

2. How well do you believe other people know you? Do they perceive you to be something or someone different from who you really are?

3. If you could do or try something that you really like, knowing that no one would make fun of you or judge you, what would you do?

4. Why do you think God made you the way he did?

THE WORLD THINKS:

This is kind of a weird one, because on one hand the world tells you to be yourself and do what you want, but the world also sends the message that you shouldn't push it so far that you don't fit in anymore. You are caught in a contradiction of feeling like you are supposed to be different but that you could pay a price because of those differences.

ACT:

Without judging people, take a few days to simply observe your friends' differences and unique characteristics. What things do your friends do that stand out to you as different? What things do your friends love that define them? See if you can encourage your friends in those differences this week. How might they feel if you both comment on and praise them for those things?

READ:

Psalm 37:4, Matthew 6:19, and Ephesians 2:10

ℕ⁰2 WHO ARE YOU AT SCHOOL?

At some point, most people have considered this question. It's somewhat foundational to how you manage to figure out the best way to navigate your high school years. At some point we all self-identify as something in school. Maybe you are an athlete and that's what defines you. Or maybe you participate in band, drama, or other artistic groups. Maybe academics are more your bent and define who you are. The reality, though, is that most of who we are at school ends up being defined by what we do. This makes sense, I guess, but it's also a little bit of a daunting thing because being "labeled" can have some negativity associated with it. Even though most things have positive traits, some opposite things often are associated with them, too.

Sometimes we are defined by others and not by our own choices. This can feel incredibly unfair—especially if the label is negative. The truth, too, is that in general who we are at school is probably only a small piece of who we actually are.

You will probably feel best, though, the more you are able to truly be yourself and not be defined by what you do or how others think of you. How do you do that? Well, I hope that during your junior year this starts happening more naturally as you spend more time doing the things that give you the most meaning, and discover and develop the gifts and talents God has given you.

THINK ABOUT:

1. What gifts and talents has God given you? How do you know, and how are you using those gifts and talents?

2. How much of what people see of you at school is really
    who you are?

3. If you could choose a few parts of your personality that
    you really like and show those to people, what would you
    want them to see? Why?

THE WORLD THINKS:

*It's OK to be defined by what you do, and you should try to
do as much as possible so you will have a better chance of
figuring out what you really like. If you want to get into a good
college, you have to be a well-rounded student, anyway. Do
things even if you don't like them, because it will pay off in the
end.*

ACT:

Is there something you wish you could do at school that you
just are too scared to attempt or haven't felt like it's the right
time to try? Step outside your comfort zone and do it. Tell
three people about it, and ask them to keep you accountable
and encourage you.

READ:

Psalm 139:1-6 and 1 Peter 2:9

℔3 WHO ARE YOU AT HOME?

Growing up, I was pretty much a hermit when I was home. I spent a lot of time in my room reading—and by "a lot of time" I mean like all the time. When I wasn't eating or doing jobs around the house, I was in my room. Because of that I would say I wasn't very present in my home, and my family jokingly called my room "The Cave." And my other role besides "cave dweller" was that of being the only boy in my family. So I did a lot of traditional guy jobs such as splitting wood, cutting the grass, washing cars, and things like that.

Now that I look back, what I regret about my high school years at home is that I wasn't really very present with my family. I don't remember having a lot of deep conversations with either of my parents or my sisters. I think I missed out on a lot of wisdom and growth that would have come from those times. Whatever your home situation may be, take time to value and invest in your relationships with your family. Down the road, you'll be happy that you did.

THINK ABOUT:

1. If you had to label your "at-home persona" in just a few words, how would you describe it?

2. How engaged are you with your family, and what things do you all like to do together?

3. What are some of the unique, specific things that you bring to your family?

4. Because God has put you in this family, what do you think your specific role is? Why?

THE WORLD THINKS:

There is a high probability your family will disappoint you, so you should work to protect yourself from that happening.

ACT:

Do something different this week with your family. If you are like me and enjoy hibernating, see what would happen if you took the time to actively engage one of your parents or another family member in a conversation. Take the time to really be present and "with" others.

READ:

Genesis 18:19, Joshua 24:15, and Zephaniah 3:17

№.4 WHO ARE YOU AT CHURCH?

I don't remember ever missing youth group in middle school or high school. (You know this already if you've read the previous books in this series.) I was at every event, camp, retreat, and all Sunday mornings and Wednesday nights. I loved my youth group and church. But I had a really different personality and role at church than I did anywhere else in my life. It was at my church that I first learned that I had some leadership skills. It was there that people began to encourage me to share what I thought. It was on retreats and at camps where I found out that I was really good at hiking and biking and that I could push myself pretty hard.

You may have a similar story—you're really involved in a youth group. I wonder who you are in that group. Depending on your personality and the size of the group, it can be easy to fade into the background and not really be known. Even though I was very involved in youth group, I wasn't fully known at my home church by other adults. I'm pretty convinced God put me in that church for a reason, though—and every time I'm home and drive past that building, I have special memories of connecting with God there.

THINK ABOUT:

1. Who are you at church? Do you have a different persona than at school?

2. How does your youth group or church impact you?

3. How many people at your youth group or church truly know who you are?

4. Why do you go to church? What do you hope to find there?

THE WORLD THINKS:

Don't waste your time going to a church or youth group. You're just going to hear a bunch of rules about what you are not supposed to do. No one there really cares about you.

ACT:

See if you can make an appointment with your church's youth pastor or senior pastor. Go in and ask them a few questions about how well they know you. Assure them that you are not trying to make them feel bad; you just want to know if you really are "known" at your church or youth group. After those potentially awkward moments, ask them to give you some advice about how to be more involved and engaged and known.

READ:

Acts 2:38, Hebrews 10:24-25, and 1 John 1:7

№.5 WHO ARE YOU WHEN YOU FEEL PAIN?

Nobody likes to feel pain. I've never really been hurt, broken anything, or seen the inside of a hospital from a patient's point of view. On one hand that is a good thing because I've lived a relatively healthy life. But there is one downside to this: Because I haven't experienced much physical pain, I don't really know how to handle it. On the emotional level, too, I haven't had anyone close to me die, nor have I had a lot of things that might cause serious emotions to happen. Again there is a downside: If and when these emotionally painful events occur, I won't have experience to help me handle them.

You may have dealt with a lot of physical or emotional pain. It's no fun. But who are you when you feel pain? Does it cause you to give up, give in, or be incapacitated? Or does it spark an inner desire to endure and grow? How do you relate to a God who allows pain to happen sometimes, and how does that experience affect your attitude toward God?

THINK ABOUT:

1. What's the worst physical pain you've experienced? How did you respond?

2. What's the worst emotional pain you've experienced? How did you respond?

3. Where did you learn how to respond to pain you feel?

4. Why do you think God allows pain to happen?

THE WORLD THINKS:

Pain bites, and your goal should be to eliminate feeling it so you don't put yourself in any situation where you could potentially have to handle any negative or painful emotions or feelings.

ACT:

Step outside yourself for a bit, and see if you can help someone else who might be going through a painful situation. How can you best comfort and care for someone? Focusing on the needs of others can give us extra strength to endure the physical or emotional pain we're experiencing.

READ:

Psalm 18:2, Romans 8:18, and 1 Corinthians 10:13

№6 WHERE DO YOU FIND YOUR SELF-WORTH?

It's an odd thing to admit, but many of us don't know how we are supposed to find our self-worth. Because of that, we get caught up looking for it in places where we likely won't find truth. We sometimes end up in unhealthy relationships because we buy into the lie that if someone "likes" us we must have worth. Or we focus so intently on one particular thing—because people pat us on the back for it—that we neglect all the other parts of our life.

I hope you have found some healthy things that provide you with a strong sense of worth. In our churches, youth group, and small groups, often other people will affirm our God-given strengths, which is a healthy thing. But that's not always the case. Self-worth is a tough thing, and figuring it out can be a long journey. At times you will have a strong sense of it and how God sees you, but other times it will have a bit more of a struggle. Keep going and look to see how God affirms those things in you.

THINK ABOUT:

1. What are three specific things you feel good about yourself?

2. How do you think God sees you right now?

3. Where do you look for affirmation? Why?

4. What are some negative places you look?

THE WORLD THINKS:

Look in yourself to find affirmation and self-worth. No one else will provide those things for you.

ACT:

Sometimes we need to spend time preparing for when we feel down. Take a piece of paper and write out three things that you like and that help you feel good about yourself, and put it in a place you can read when you feel low.

READ:

Proverbs 28:6, Matthew 16:26, Ephesians 4:32, and Colossians 3:12-14

№7 WHO ARE YOU WITH YOUR FRIENDS?

I had a friend in high school who had the potential to get me in a lot of trouble. I say "potential" because we were always right on the edge of doing things that would have gone bad for us if we'd been caught. It wasn't a lot of illegal stuff—mostly some pretty major pranks or just being places we shouldn't be. With my friend I was sort of a follower. But I was one of the chief followers in our group. I was always up for anything as long as someone else was coming up with the plan.

I think I struggled saying no to some of the things we did because I really needed those friendships. I grew up on an island and went to the school with the same people year after year, so I had a limited number of possibilities for friends. I know that my friends all liked having me around, but I still sort of wonder what they really thought of me. I know that my relationship with God and my faith didn't really have much to do with our friendships. I compartmentalized so much of my faith and life. It's something I look back on with regret because it really took me years to start having deep faith conversations with friends.

Fortunately, you can walk down a different path. You can start having Jesus-centered conversations with friends, and your life can demonstrate what it means to place your faith and trust in Jesus. Being yourself and being a solid Christ-follower can go hand in hand.

THINK ABOUT:

1. What is your go-to role in most of your friendships?

2. How much of a role does your faith play in your friendships?

3. How scared are you of being alone? How does that shape the way you interact with your friends?

4. What are some parts of your personality that you wish you could expose more to your friends?

THE WORLD THINKS:

You need friends, especially at school because it is an unsafe and scary place. Don't do anything to ruin your friendships. Go along with what other people want because you need them.

ACT:

Spend some time with one or more of your friends and ask them some questions about yourself. What do they like about you? Why do they think you are friends? How comfortable do they feel being themselves around you? How do they think your friendships can grow deeper? What role does faith play in your friendships?

READ:

1 Samuel 16:7, John 15:15, and 1 Thessalonians 1:4-10

ɴᴏ.8 WHO ARE YOU WHEN YOU ARE ALONE?

I like to be alone—I like space and time to myself. Growing up, that meant I spent a lot of time in my room or out on my boat. Generally, I was reading in both those places. As an adult, my introverted patterns have continued, and I find that I need space away from people in order to recharge my batteries. This is especially true after a big chunk of time with a large group. You may be that way after a day at school, a big event at church or time with your friends. That's one way that being alone isn't a bad thing.

But there is a downside to it as well. When I'm alone, there isn't anyone around me to keep me doing the right things, encourage me to make good choices, or bring me back when I go astray. The negative side of being alone is isolation, and it's often during these times that my struggles come out. You may be the same as me and find that you struggle with things when you have too much alone time. I've heard many times from people in my life that integrity is making the right choices when you are alone. God walks alongside you in all of your decisions and in the times you're alone, and he's ready to help you make the right choices, even if it's not always a struggle you win.

THINK ABOUT:

1. When do you enjoy being alone? What things do you like to do when you're alone?

2. When do you find that alone time is the healthiest for you? the hardest for you?

3. Are there things that you do alone that you would be ashamed if others knew about? You don't have to list them here, but how does your answer to that question make you feel?

4. Do you believe God is always with you, or are there times you feel alone?

THE WORLD THINKS:

Ultimately, you need to worry about you and take care of you. No one else really cares about you, so spending time alone and not relying on other people is something you need to do a lot in order to get good at it.

ACT:

This week, spend some time alone. Take a journal and find a three-hour chunk of time to sit and think about how it feels to be alone. Ditch the phone and everything else that distracts you—just be by yourself. Write about how you feel.

READ:

Mark 1:35, Mark 9:2, and John 6:15

№9 WHAT GIFTS AND TALENTS DID GOD GIVE YOU?

Sometimes thinking about gifts and talents feels like we are patting ourselves on the back. The reality is that God has give all of us talents and skills, and when we become followers of Christ, we also receive spiritual gifts—and it's OK to stoked about all of this. Early in my life I realized that I had an aptitude for understanding computers better than most other people. That is my way of stating that I had some geek tendencies.

For a while I felt like the best way to use those gifts was to attend college, get a computer science degree, and go work at a big computer company. But there was one problem. Although God gifted me with the ability to grasp the usefulness and importance of computers, I wasn't given the gift of math or processing power. So after one semester I stopped trying to do computer things.

Today I'm a youth pastor who uses technology for a lot of different things. I know God has suited me to do exactly what I'm doing. You may not have figured out what your gifts and talents are yet. That's OK. For some of us it takes a bit longer. But you have them, and figuring out what they are is an important step in understanding your role and place in this world.

THINK ABOUT:

1. What are some gifts and talents you think God may have given you? How do you know?

2. What are some things you think you are good at? Do you have a sense of what God might be calling you to do with those gifts and talents?

3. If you could pick gifts or talents different from the ones you have, what would they be and why?

THE WORLD THINKS:

Some people have a lot of gifts and talents, and they will likely be wildly successful. But that group is small. Most people aren't given anything and just have to work really hard just to get by.

ACT:

Chances are good you have some people in your life who know you pretty well. Ask two of them to tell you which gifts and talents they see in your life. See if they can give you some advice about what you could do with those gifts and talents.

READ:

Matthew 25:14-30, 1 Corinthians 14:12, and Colossians 3:23-24

№.10 IF YOU COULD CHANGE THINGS ABOUT YOURSELF, WHAT WOULD YOU CHANGE?

As I discussed in the previous reading, God made us and gave us specific gifts for a reason. But often we don't use those gifts in the ways he intended—and this is something I'd like to change in my own life. I have always been pretty good at figuring things out, and I generally can walk into a lot of situations and fairly quickly know how to solve whatever problem is in front of me. Unfortunately, that often leads me to being a little bit lazy and a bit of a procrastinator. I know God doesn't appreciate me waiting until the last minute to use the gifts he's given me. That's the first thing I would change about myself.

Another thing I'd love to change is my inability to focus on things when I need to. Again, I believe God has given me a pretty decent brain and the ability to get things done, but often I'm distracted and unfocused, and it takes me way more time to get things done than it should. The final thing I'd change is the measure of selfishness I feel toward my time. I sometimes just want to be by myself and do my own thing instead of fully embracing my friends and family and being a selfless person.

Do you have a similar list in your own life? Wanting to change isn't a sign that you're unhappy with who God made you to be, and it isn't an indication of low self-esteem, either. It's the recognition that you're an individual capable of growth and change and maturity. That's such an important part of your faith journey.

THINK ABOUT:

1. What are some things you want to change about yourself, and why?

2. How do you think God reacts when you don't wisely use the gifts he's given you?

3. Why do you want to make these changes? What could you do differently?

THE WORLD THINKS:

Just be you. Don't worry about what anyone else thinks, and if you don't want to do something, don't do it. Pretty soon you're going to be an adult, anyway, and you won't have to do what other people tell you. It's all about you, so you shouldn't worry about what anyone else thinks.

ACT:

This week, begin the journey of changing a habit. If there is something in your life you want to stop doing, come up with a plan to change it. Write it down, tell other people about it, and work hard to focus on changing that one thing.

READ:

1 Corinthians 3:16, 2 Corinthians 5:17-21, and Colossians 3:3-4

SECTION 2

WHO DO OTHERS SAY YOU ARE?

This wasn't a big enough deal to me when I was in high school. These days, though, I think a lot about how others could have had a different view of who I was during my teenage years. If I could go back and do it over, I would make sure that my heart for people and my concern for those who were hurting would have been more apparent my junior year. I wish people would have said that they saw positive things in me and that it was so clear how much I loved and cared for others.

But I don't think that side of me was obvious to people back then. I'm pretty sure that my junior classmates, parents, and others saw me as someone who didn't really knowing who he was and someone who didn't really think about other people. I think they saw me as a goofy kid who didn't know what he was all about and who struggled with recognizing how he fit into the world. I would have benefited from more affirmations about my gifts or talents and how I had something to contribute to society.

№ 11 WHO DO YOUR FRIENDS SAY YOU ARE?

What words might your friends use to describe you? Would they be accurate? How well do your friends know you? If I think back to my junior year of high school, I know my friends would have said that I was loyal, always fun, and up for anything. I think they really knew me, and I felt totally comfortable with them because they accepted me for who I was and I could be open, honest, and real around them.

If this is your story, congratulations! It's great to have these kinds of friends—especially if they're followers of Christ, too. Invest in these amazing friendships. Value the people who accept you just as you are—your successes, your failures, your strengths, and your flaws.

But it's likely some of you have a different experience: Either you don't have close friends or you don't feel like you totally can be yourself around them. It's hard for you to open up, and you struggle to be fully you. I want to encourage you—this may be your story today, but you can build those kinds of relationships when you get older. You'll have more opportunities to build friendships with people who will support and encourage and know you.

The reality is that we are all concerned about what our friends think of us because those friendships really matter. Our friends play a large part in our lives and how we feel about ourselves. It's important to surround ourselves with people who truly know us and genuinely care about our best interest.

THINK ABOUT:

1. Who do your friends say you are? Why do they say that?

2. What role do you have in your circle of friends?

3. If you are having a rough day or a tough situation, which of your friends do you turn to—and why?

4. Do your friends think your faith and trust in Jesus is strong? Why or why not?

THE WORLD THINKS:

The world has a couple of thoughts on friends. On one hand we are cautioned to not get too close to anyone, and on the other hand we hear that friends are more important than family. Both of these extremes can be risky.

ACT:

How can you be a better friend to people in your life? Think of three friends, and come up with a list of specific things you could do to help them out. Then do it.

READ:

Proverbs 13:20, John 15:12-15, and 1 Corinthians 15:33

⒏12 WHO DO YOUR PARENTS SAY YOU ARE?

Thinking about your relationship with your parents may bring up some difficult and tough thoughts. Whether your relationship with them is strong or weak, frustrating or encouraging, you are still shaped by what you hear from them about who you are. Sometimes these messages are subtle; sometimes they're blatant. You might hear over and over again that you are the baby of the family, so they treat you like a child who will never grow up. Or you might be the firstborn who is considered responsible and has leadership skills—and your parents frequently remind you of this.

Chances are good that at least once you have heard your parents verbalize how they genuinely see you. Those may be special, life-giving moments as your parents speak truths about the gifts and talents God has given you. Or in their own brokenness and hurt, they may say things that aren't true and tear you down. As difficult as this next statement may be to read, it's true: *God has put you in the specific family where you are*—it isn't always easy, but as you trust God you can learn, grow, and mature.

THINK ABOUT:

1. What things do you hear your parents say about you?

2. What do you wish your parents knew about you—or what messages do you wish they spoke to you? Why?

3. How much do you believe your parents truly understand who you are?

4. How do you think God might want you to serve and love your parents?

THE WORLD THINKS:

Parents will disappoint you. They are hurting, selfish people just like you are, and you should expect to be hurt by them. Don't worry—soon you'll be out of their house and won't have to deal with them anymore.

ACT:

This week, flip things around and do something totally different with your parents. Tell them what good things you see in them. Pave the way for this kind of encouragement to flow both directions by doing it first. This might mean writing a letter, telling them in person, or leaving a long message on their voice mail. The goal is to share with your parents some of the good things you see in them.

READ:

Psalm 127:3-5, Psalm 138:8, and Matthew 5:13

№13 WHO DO YOUR TEACHERS SAY YOU ARE?

All of us to a certain extent play some sort of role at school. We decide that there are particular things we can do that will protect us and allow us to feel comfortable and safe. You might be the student who is always helpful and willing to answer questions, or you could be the exact opposite: the back-of-the-classroom type who just wants to get through the day without being noticed. For the most part, teachers are aware of who students are and really do care about you. (I say this as a former teacher!) That's why they started teaching in the first place.

Do you ever wonder what your teachers think about you? Spend some time listening to what your teachers say to you (and to your classmates). They may be encouragers who say things that build you up. Or they may be pushers who know you could be doing so much more, so they push you to succeed. Some of your teachers may be followers of Jesus, but many may not be. As a Christ-follower, you are called to be a light to the world, and that includes being a light to your school and teachers. Let your faith shine through as you spend time in their classrooms learning, discussing, interacting, and listening.

THINK ABOUT:

1. What are some things you have heard your teachers say about you?

2. How well do you believe your teachers know who you really are?

3. Do you believe you are known as the real you at school, or are you acting a part?

4. How might God be calling you to be a light to your teachers and school?

THE WORLD THINKS:

A lot of teachers don't care about you. They work tough jobs and can't wait for the day and the school year to be over. So don't expect too much from them.

ACT:

This week, encourage a teacher. Imagine how it would make a teacher feel if you sent them a note thanking them for what they do and the way they do it to really care for you as a student. I bet it would make a huge difference. (Again, I say this as a former teacher!)

READ:

Exodus 33:17, 1 Chronicles 25:8, Ecclesiastes 12:12-13, and Luke 6:40

™14 WHO DO YOUR COACHES SAY YOU ARE?

Not everyone reading this is an athlete. But perhaps you've been on a team at some point in your life. I'm not a great athlete at all, but I competed in soccer, football, tennis, and wrestling for a number of years. I particularly remember that my tennis coach was glad I was on his team, but that he was fairly convinced I just wasn't ever going to be one of his star players. He said that I was good to have on the practice squad, but I just didn't have it in me to work hard enough to be very good. I enjoyed tennis and my teammates, and I liked my coach—although I was also a little scared of him!

Sports may be a bigger part of your high school life than it was for me, and you may find that it is on your teams and through your coaches and teammates that you have learned a lot about yourself and who you are. Maybe your coaches have helped you discover skills you didn't realize you had, or they've encouraged you to become a more disciplined athlete, which has allowed you to become a more disciplined person overall. I learned a long time ago that God gave me just enough talent to be OK at most things but not an all-star at anything athletic. But I'm OK with that.

THINK ABOUT:

1. What have you heard from coaches (or P.E. teachers) that you think is true about yourself?

2. Do you think your coaches have accurately assessed who you are as a person from what they have seen at practice and games?

3. What are some things that you have learned from coaches about yourself?

4. What type of physical gifts and talents did God give you? How do you use them to honor him?

THE WORLD THINKS:

Sports are all about talent—and you either have it or you don't. If you have it, you will be successful and liked—and if you don't, no one will care.

ACT:

If you have a sport that you like to play, talk to one of your coaches this week and see if they can assess your gifts and skills and what you need to work on. If you feel comfortable, ask them how they think those skills can translate into other areas of your life.

READ:

Deuteronomy 31:6, Psalm 37:23-24, Ephesians 6:13, Philippians 4:13, and 1 Timothy 4:8

ᴺᴼ·15 WHO DOES YOUR YOUTH GROUP SAY YOU ARE?

My youth group helped me learn a lot of truth about who I was. At school I was quieter and more shy and definitely not a leader, but at youth group I was given all kinds of opportunities to shine and be successful.

I know my youth group would say that I was fun to be around and that I added a lot to the spice and life of our group. I was always up for fun and adventure and could generally be counted on to provide some comic relief on trips and activities. People in my group, though, also would probably say that they weren't really sure about my faith and the depth of my relationship with God. That wasn't something I was encouraged to express very often, so it was something that was a lot more internal and less visible for me.

You may be really involved in a youth group, like I was. If that's true, think about how the people there are a part of your spiritual journey and life. Do they truly know you? But if you don't have a youth group that you feel connected to, consider finding one where you can get involved, attend, and serve. You only have a couple of years of school left, but it's never too late to get connected.

THINK ABOUT:

1. What are some truths you think your youth group would say about you?

2. What are some things you wish other members of your youth group knew about you?

3. How much do you value your youth group being a safe place where you can grow in your faith? What can get in the way of growth happening?

4. How has God used people in your youth group to speak truth into your life?

THE WORLD THINKS:

You will eventually get bored of going to church—and besides, you only go there because your parents make you. What do you really think you are getting out of it?

ACT:

If your faith in Christ is something that is important to you, make some key decisions about how you will live it out. Talk to your youth leader about how you can grow in your faith, and see if they can give you some tips and ideas that will help you. Look for opportunities to serve that will benefit the whole group.

READ:

Matthew 5:14, Romans 6:18, Ephesians 2:6, and 1 Peter 2:5

ℕ⁰ 16 WHO DO YOUR ONLINE FRIENDS SAY YOU ARE?

I was thinking recently about how when I send text messages, it must be hard for some people to figure out what I'm trying to say. I use emoticons to give some sort of "feeling" to my messages, but I think they're still hard to read. The way I see it, social media sites provide so many opportunities to miscommunicate, er, connect with so many people.

On Facebook® I try to be funny and get people to reply to my messages. This feels so passive-aggressive because I say things hoping to get a response—a difficult task to accomplish repeatedly. I'm guessing that my online friends would have a pretty different view of my life than how it is in reality since I only show them most of the good stuff!

What about for you? Do your online friends truly know you? Or do they know a side of you that doesn't show up at youth group or around classmates or family members? Because I grew up in the pre-Internet dark ages, I didn't have to deal with how I acted online or what I revealed to people on the Internet. But I understand the value of consistency and being the same person wherever I am and whichever people I'm talking with.

THINK ABOUT:

1. What do you believe your online friends think of you?

2. How do you try to portray yourself online? Is it an accurate depiction of who you really are?

3. Do you sometimes find yourself spending more time with your online friends than your real-life friends? Why or why not?

4. How much do your online friends see of your faith in Jesus? Is that something that's important for you to share with them? Why or why not?

THE WORLD THINKS:

It's OK to be a different person in different spaces. Everyone needs the freedom to be whoever they want to be wherever they want to be it.

ACT:

A couple of years ago, one of my friends decided to challenge himself to personally meet as many of his online friends as he could. So he started meeting people at coffee shops, calling people on the phone, and building more connections between those lives. Do that this week. Reach out to some of your social media friends and build some real-life connections.

READ:

Proverbs 13:20, Proverbs 22:24-25, and Colossians 3:12-14

№17 WHO DOES YOUR BOSS SAY YOU ARE?

Bosses are interesting people, and I can remember three of my bosses growing up. My first boss was at a Mexican food restaurant where I worked for two days. I don't even think he knew my name because I was just filling in for something. He said I worked hard, but that's it. My second boss was at the pool where I worked as a lifeguard. That boss said I was always on time but would probably question the amount of work I actually did, seeing how I spent a significant portion of my time lying in a lounge chair.

My third boss was on a farm where I helped "hay" a field and pack the bales into the barn. It was really hard work, and I never complained. That boss would say I worked really hard, and he would take me back anytime.

Maybe you haven't had a job yet, so this is all about thinking how you want a boss to see you and how well you do your job. Or perhaps you've had jobs and you've had bosses tell you some things that they see in you. If your faith in Jesus is important to you, then it ought to shape how you work with and relate to your boss. That person should be able to see something different in you than employees who aren't followers of Christ. Do they? Will they?

THINK ABOUT:

1. What have you heard from a boss about yourself? Was it good or bad?

2. What do you wish that your boss knew about you?

3. If you haven't had a boss yet, what are two key traits you would want to have and be rewarded for as an employee?

4. How do you believe God wants you to relate to your boss and your workplace? In what ways can your faith influence how you act?

THE WORLD THINKS:

Work is lame and we just do it because we have to make money and pay the bills. You shouldn't expect much from your bosses—in fact, you actually need to protect yourself from being too vulnerable because it could get you fired.

ACT:

If you have a job now, think about specific characteristics you would love to be known for as an employee. This week, work on making them your priority at work. If you don't have a job yet, take that same list and see if you can make them priorities in your everyday life.

READ:

Romans 13:1-7, Titus 3:1-2, Hebrews 13:17, and 1 Peter 5:5

№.18 WHO DOES YOUR WALLET SAY YOU ARE?

In countless sermons over the years, I've heard it said that anyone could see exactly what I cared about simply by looking at how I spend my money. How accurate is that statement? Well, when I went back and looked at my most recent bank statement, I found it to be true. I spent a lot of money on coffee, student loans, eating out with my family, and fun activities—all of which are important to me.

You may only have a little money from gifts, an allowance, or a part-time job. Chances are good, though, that how you spend your money says a lot about what you value. Jesus talks about money more than almost any other topic in the New Testament. I think that means it's something he cares a lot about. You may have a lot of money or very little of it, but regardless of how much you start with, how you spend it says a lot about your priorities.

THINK ABOUT:

1. What are the last three things you spent money on? What does that tell you?

2. If you had $250 right now, what would you do with it? Why?

3. How much does money shape what you are thinking about for your future?

4. How do you think Jesus would want you to spend your money? Why?

THE WORLD THINKS:

Money brings happiness—simple as that. When you have more of it, you are happier.

ACT:

For one week, write down an exact report of how you spend your money. Don't put anything into categories; just do a simple ledger with an explanation of what it was and how much you spent. At the end of the week, give that ledger to a friend (or even better, someone who doesn't know you very well), and ask that person to determine what appears important to you based on how you spent your money.

READ:

Psalm 112:5, Proverbs 21:5, Jeremiah 22:13, and Luke 14:28-30

№.19 WHO DOES YOUR PAST SAY YOU ARE?

It's easy to hang on to the past. Sometimes we do this because our past was great and filled with a lot of wonderful memories. We attempt to re-create these events over and over, instead of pursuing new opportunities and new dreams; we become hooked on reliving the past. On the other end of the spectrum, sometimes we hang on to the past because it was difficult and filled with painful memories that seem to hold us captive. We want to move on and leave those things behind, but we feel trapped; our mind plays them over and over and over.

The truth is that much of our past follows us as we get older, but our past doesn't have to define us. We can move beyond the bad things (and the good things, too) and work to live in the present. Thinking about how you are shaped by your past will help you work through who you are today and who you can become tomorrow.

God can heal and redeem the painful moments. God also can give us new memories that surpass the greatest ones from the past. God uses our past to shape us, and I hope that you've had the opportunity to walk through some of yours with other Christians that you trust.

THINK ABOUT:

1. What are some things from your past you wish you could forget?

2. What are some things from your past you wish you could repeat?

3. How do you think God might use and redeem the tough, difficult, painful things from your past?

4. When good and bad things happen to you, where do you think God is? Is God equally present during good and bad times? Why or why not?

THE WORLD THINKS:

Who you are today is shaped by your past, and you can never get away from the things that happened there. If you messed up, that will always be with you. You'll have to deal with the consequences on your own.

ACT:

Write a list of five major things you remember from your past—both negative and positive things. What did you learn from each of those events or moments? If you have a trusted Christian adult in your life, ask that person to help you make sense of how God might be using some of your past—or how God might use those moments in the future.

READ:

Isaiah 1:18, Isaiah 43:18-19, Acts 22:1-29, and
Philippians 3:12-14

⚏·20 WHO DO YOUR HABITS SAY YOU ARE?

I was thinking recently about my daughter and her bedroom. My daughter is only 7 years old, and her room generally looks like it was hit with a tornado. Her habits reveal what does matter and doesn't matter—she doesn't have a high value for "neatness" in her room, but she does value friends and play time. If you walked by her room at any point that she has a friend over, you would see that they are really focused on having fun—and the mess doesn't seem to bother them as much as it bothers me.

I'm slightly different from her. In many cases, I like life to be neat and orderly, without a lot of surprises. I value plans and information and generally don't do really well with spontaneity and disorder. My habits follow me into my church, too. I am a pastor in a denomination that believes things should be done in a particular order—and when things get a little out of sync, it just feels wrong.

We are all capable of developing good habits and bad habits. A good habit would be taking a shower every day and washing your hair. A bad habit would be taking a shower once every two weeks. (That kid was part of my youth group long ago.) Our lives are filled with numerous habits, and they say a lot about what is important to us and what we value.

THINK ABOUT:

1. What are some of your good habits? What habits in your life are bad? Which are easier to develop, and why?

2. In your Christian walk, what are some habits that help you draw near to God? How did you develop these habits?

3. Have you been trying to put in place any healthy habits that have been difficult to get going? What are they, and how might another person help you in this quest?

THE WORLD THINKS:

Do whatever you want, however you want. Yes, you are defined by what you do, but don't let anyone else tell you what habits are good or not.

ACT:

Most healthy habits require time and effort; they don't happen overnight or automatically. Want a good strategy for starting a new good habit or stopping a bad one? Write out a detailed plan of action and share it with two people. Consider specific steps or choices that you will help you begin that healthy habit—or end that unhealthy one!

READ:

Romans 12:2, Ephesians 5:1-2, 1 Timothy 5:13, and Hebrews 10:24-25

SECTION 3

WHO DOES JESUS SAY YOU ARE?

I have this 20-year-old bookmark sitting on my desk at work. It is covered in some encouraging one-word thoughts about who I was and am, written by some people I was really close to at that point in my life. The other day I was reading those thoughts, and I started to pray that Jesus would make all those qualities more evident in my life. I know that Jesus has a high value of who I am. I've actually always felt that—even in middle school when I felt displaced and not liked. I had a sense that Jesus loved me. I knew that I had worth and that I was made for a purpose.

Jesus has the same sense of purpose and belief in you. This year, it's critical that you know Jesus loves you and believes in you—that he loves the gifts God gave you and is fully committed to cheering you on as you use them. Figuring out the truths of what God says about you and holding tightly to them will help you as you continue to grow, mature, and walk through all the difficulties and joys of life.

№21 YOU ARE LOVED

Even when you don't feel it, you need to know that Jesus loves you. You may be at a point in your life where you don't feel that many people love you. Well, Jesus does and always will.

You may encounter a season of life when you are struggling to believe this simple truth. The beauty of the Christian faith is that when we struggle the most to believe, God does something amazing: He gives us the ability to stand upon other people's beliefs and faith. We can simply say, "I'm doubting" and allow the faith of others to be "enough" for us at that point.

This often happens for people when tragedy strikes and they don't know how to respond to God. At those moments, we often are best served sitting and being with people who do believe. So remember that you are loved by God, and even when you don't believe it, others can hold this truth for you.

THINK ABOUT:

1. How does it feel to say, "Jesus loves me"?

2. Have you experienced times when you haven't believed that Jesus loves you? How do you respond during those periods of doubt?

3. How does knowing Jesus loves you change the way you view the world, your place in it, and your future?

THE WORLD THINKS:

Many people learn the song Jesus Loves Me, *but no one really believes that it makes any sort of difference in anyone's lives.*

ACT:

Find a Christian adult this week and ask about times they have doubted that Jesus loved them. Ask them how they made it through those seasons.

READ:

John 3:16, Romans 8:38-39, and 1 Corinthians 13:1-3

№. 22 YOU ARE PERFECTLY MADE

Nick Vujicic was born without any arms or legs, yet he knows that he is perfectly made. Nick is probably one of the most influential Christian speakers today, a man who shares incredible stories about God's love and how Jesus transformed his tough circumstance. He speaks all over the world and also does activities that you would never expect someone with his limitations to do, including participating in several different sports and being able to type. I have never met Nick, but I have heard him speak and know that he believes God made him this way for a specific purpose: so that he could be an influence in the lives of millions.

At first glance, many people would doubt that Nick is "perfectly made." But that is exactly what he believes. And I'm convinced that God knew exactly what he was doing when he made you, too. All the hairs on your head, the freckles on your nose, and the toes on your feet—God has put you together for a specific purpose, and you are perfect in God's eyes.

THINK ABOUT:

1. How do you feel when you read the words "You are perfectly made"?

2. If you could change some things about your body, what would you change? Why?

3. Does hearing Nick's story change how you view yourself? Why or why not?

THE WORLD THINKS:

Some people are just born more perfect than others, and stories like Nick's are not normal. You probably have flaws, and that is proof that no one really created you.

ACT:

Go to lifewithoutlimbs.com and read through Nick's testimony. Think about the limitations you believe you have, and consider how you can rethink your own struggles and ask God to use you exactly how he made you.

READ:

Matthew 10:30 and Ephesians 1:4-5

№23 YOU ARE BEAUTIFUL (OR HANDSOME)

I wonder how many of us look in the mirror and honestly think, "I'm so beautiful (or so handsome)." Maybe we're capable of seeing that on some days—but struggle with it on other days. The reality is that we often view ourselves as if we were looking at one of those super-magnification mirrors—the ones in which you can see every pore and flaw in your face. Those mirrors tend to distort your actual appearance and can make your face look pretty scary.

It's frustrating to me that in our culture today, we judge our beauty on how we compare against countless movie stars, magazine images, and billboards. What drives me nuts the most is that all of us know that every one of those images is an airbrushed, glamorized version of the actual person. We know that the photos aren't entirely real or accurate, but we still compare ourselves against what we see.

The cool reality is that God has made us all beautiful in his eyes, and it's only the world that has perverted the truth about beauty and good looks. You deserve to be freed from the false reality the world has sold you and know that you are beautiful (or handsome).

THINK ABOUT:

1. How does it make you feel to hear someone say, "You are beautiful (or handsome)"?

2. What is the first thing you think when you look at yourself in a mirror?

3. How might you and your friends help each other to have a healthier and more biblical view of beauty?

THE WORLD THINKS:

There are beautiful people, and then there are the rest of us. You know which category you fall into pretty easily. That's just the way it is (though you're welcome to spend all your money on clothes, makeup, surgeries, and gym memberships in an attempt to become more beautiful or handsome).

ACT:

I know this is a tough sell. It's hard to try to believe something different from what the world tells you. So this week, focus on other people. Spend time complimenting your friends and encouraging them in how God has made them. Try to move away from commenting on outward appearance and instead give compliments based on the whole person and character.

READ:

Proverbs 31:30, Ezekiel 16:14, and 1 Peter 3:3-4

NO. 24 YOU ARE WONDERFULLY MADE

I was thinking the other day about a song lyric from a worship tune that says, "Wonderful, so wonderful, is your unfailing love." I will be honest: The word *wonderful* generally doesn't appear much in my vocabulary. I'm not sure why, because it clearly is a great description of how amazed I should be at all the things God has made. The sunset is wonderful. I'm sure the sunrise (which I never see because I can't wake up early enough) is equally wonderful. The way God created my daughter to laugh is amazing and wonderful.

Unfortunately, I think the deep sense of wonder is fading in our society. With the Internet and information being so readily available, it's hard to have that sense of wonder about things because they're easy to dissect and explain.

Years ago I read a great book by Mike Yaconelli called *A Dangerous Wonder*, in which he describes a scene of his young nephew experiencing snow for the first time. It was more than the young child's senses could handle, so to take it all in he simply fell into it. For him the sense of "wonder" took over and literally enveloped him as he experienced it.

THINK ABOUT:

1. What does the word *wonderful* mean to you?

2. How does it feel to think that God created you and sees you as wonderfully made?

3. What are some things that you would say are "wonderful" and make you think of God?

THE WORLD THINKS:

There is a science behind why sunsets are as pretty as they are. It's not God at all; more than likely your beautiful sunset is a result of pollution.

ACT:

Make a list of things that you think are beautiful and point you to God. Put that list on your mirror in your bathroom, and pray thanks through it each morning.

READ:

Psalm 105:2, Psalm 139:13-14, and Isaiah 9:6

№.25 YOU ARE GIFTED

Some of us are really good at giving gifts. We love to buy or make things for other people, and when they open their presents we feel a rush of excitement because that's what makes us tick. Others of us are really good at receiving gifts. We love to open presents, and it makes us feel good when others give things to us. On many occasions we are surprised at how the person who gave us a gift knew exactly what we wanted. Their "knowing" us is as meaningful as the gift itself because it shows they really care about who we are. Gifts make us feel special, valued, and appreciated.

All of us have received gifts from God. For some of us, our gifts are pretty clear and easy to see. We may be good at some particular thing and we're using that gift already to serve God and to serve others. But maybe you haven't figured out exactly what your gifts are yet. Or maybe you know you have gifts that don't necessarily line up with who you are right now.

I found later in my life that I was really good at public speaking and telling stories in front of large crowds. That's an ironic gift because in high school I was so shy and terrified to ever be up in front of a group and talking. So if you don't really see what your gifts are right now or how God can use them, you might simply need to wait until it's time for you to fully understand and use them.

THINK ABOUT:

1. What are some things you believe God has gifted you in? How can you use those gifts to serve God and to serve others?

2. How does it make you feel to say, "God has given me some gifts"? Do you believe it? Why or why not?

3. Are there particular things you do that when you do them you feel like God smiles?

THE WORLD THINKS:

Everyone has talents. They don't come from anything or anyone.

ACT:

Think about how you can affirm gifts that you see in other people this week. Choose a couple of friends, your parents, or other adults in your life, and affirm them verbally or via notes. Talk about the gifts that you see them displaying and how clear it is that God has gifted them.

READ:

Luke 11:13, Acts 1:4, Romans 6:23, Romans 12:6, and James 1:17

☰ NO.26 YOU ARE TRUSTED

All of us want to be trusted more. You are probably at a place in your life where you are negotiating what trust looks like with your parents. This is the year of your life where a lot of trust starts being transferred as you have likely demonstrated that you are a trustworthy person. Or maybe you have made some mistakes; some of that trust from your parents has been taken back and you feel like you have to earn it again.

A great resource for understanding how this trust thing works is your Bible. God is incredibly consistent in the Bible, and we can learn a lot about how consistency breeds more trust by following his lead. All of us want to be consistent and to have people know how we will respond in all situations. We feel good when people believe in us—and frustrated when we lose that.

THINK ABOUT:

1. How much do you believe your parents or guardians trust you?

2. What are ways you have worked to earn their trust? How have you lost their trust?

3. In your Christian walk, how trustworthy has God been to you?

THE WORLD THINKS:

Trust is something that you have to be very careful with. People are out to just meet their own needs, so they generally are not very trustworthy.

ACT:

One thing you can do to demonstrate trust is to show your parents that you can be consistent. You might want to put together a "you chart" that has chores, tasks, schedules, and other things on it and give it to them so that they know what and when you are doing things. You can update it weekly so they will always have an updated schedule. Try it for three weeks and see how they trust you.

READ:

Psalm 13:5, Psalm 22:8, Psalm 28:7, Proverbs 3:5-6, and Luke 16:10

№.27 YOU ARE REDEEMED

My dad is an alcoholic. He led a pretty tough life, and alcohol was a big part of that. But the good news is that he has been sober for more than 20 years. The thing that was such a huge stumbling block in his life has been taken away. But all alcoholics will tell you that it is a daily struggle to remain sober and focused on the path ahead of them.

When I think about the word *redeemed*, I think about my dad. He could have just kept drinking and his life likely would have continued to go down an unhealthy path, but through God's grace and transforming power he was able to stop drinking and has stayed sober for many years. Redemption simply means taking something that was damaged and making it good again. Throughout the Bible you see God doing this with his people when he steps in, changes the situation they're in, frees them from bondage, slavery, and struggles, and brings them back to him.

We experience God's redemption when we place our faith and trust in Jesus. If you've already made that decision, you know it's the best choice you've ever made. If you haven't taken that step yet, I encourage you to do so—to experience a new life and redemption from God.

THINK ABOUT:

1. What are some stories of redemption you have seen in your life?

2. Why is God in the business of redeeming people?

3. What can you learn from a God who makes "all things new" with his people? How does that encourage you to live?

THE WORLD THINKS:

For the most part, redemption is not real. If you have messed up your life, there is a high probability it will just stay messed up. That's the harsh reality of life.

ACT:

Often we hear stories of redemption when people share their testimony. Ask a couple of Christ-following adults in your life this week to share with you their testimony about how God has redeemed them.

READ:

Exodus 6:6, Deuteronomy 15:15, Psalm 34:22, and Galatians 3:13

ℕ⁰.28 YOU ARE HOLY

I do a lot of baptisms in my church. As a part of those services, I take water and put it on the head of the child three times and say, "I baptize you in the name of the Father, Son, and Holy Spirit." If you look at the verses for today's reading, you see God being proclaimed as "holy" in many places. God's chosen people, the Israelites, were constantly told in the Old Testament that they had to do things in particular ways in order to "be holy"—a big deal because God could not interact with an "unholy" people. So they had laws about everything, all set up to keep them from being unholy or impure.

In the New Testament we see Jesus coming as a conclusion and answer to this law—through his death and resurrection we can be made holy. But many of us struggle daily with unholy or unworthy thoughts, actions, words, and deeds, making us feel like we aren't able to go to God. As a longtime youth pastor, I often find it pretty easy to tell when students are struggling with things because they may stop coming to church—they don't feel right about being there when they are struggling with stuff. But I want you to know how false that is. When you struggle, church is exactly where you need to be!

THINK ABOUT:

1. What does it mean to you when you hear "you are holy"?

2. How does it make you feel when you do things that you know are against what God wants you to do?

3. What are some action steps you could put into place that would help you to turn away from things that you know are not good for you?

THE WORLD THINKS:

No one is holy. Everyone fails.

ACT:

I'm not sure how much time we all think about being holy. But for the next few days, I want you to really focus on it. What would it look like if you committed to making sure that in all things you were honoring God—in your speech, thoughts, writing, and actions? Come up with an action plan, write it down, and see how you do.

READ:

Leviticus 11:44, Psalm 99:5, Philippians 4:4-9, and 1 Peter 1:15-16

№.29 YOU ARE FORGIVEN

I remember hearing a story back in high school about a guy who was caught living like a cannibal here in the United States. He had body parts in his freezer and was living off of them. The story's twist, though, happened in prison, where he became a Christian. The issue we discussed at youth group was how comfortable we were, knowing that this guy who had murdered and eaten people was going to be in heaven with us. We had a lot of conversation about this and various answers were offered, but generally speaking everyone felt like his sins were so serious that God had to somehow treat him differently than God treated us.

That story, of course, was a simple setup for my youth pastor to say that we were wrong and that God doesn't treat any sin differently—repentance and forgiveness and freedom from our past is the same for everyone and every sin. But I'll be honest and say the idea still felt weird. Even now as an adult, I find myself treating different sins as being more of a big deal than others. But God doesn't look at it that way. There is simply "holy" and "unholy," and sin falls into the second category. Through Christ, those sins can be forgiven and we can be freed.

THINK ABOUT:

1. Do you think some sins are worse than others? Why or why not?

2. If you were God, how would you go about forgiving people?

3. How hard is it for you to forgive people that have hurt you?

THE WORLD THINKS:

You should be slow to forgive people because they will likely just hurt you again. And even if you forgive, definitely don't forget. That person probably will do the exact same thing to you down the road.

ACT:

You have probably been hurt by people, and maybe it's been tough to forgive them. This week, think about someone you're holding a grudge against because he or she has hurt you. It's time to do what God has done for you and forgive without any stipulations. Do this by telling that person that you offer forgiveness, or just offer that forgiveness in your own heart—let it go and forgive.

READ:

Exodus 34:9, Psalm 32:1, Psalm 78:38, Daniel 9:9, and Matthew 6:14-15

ᴺᴼ·30 YOU HAVE HOPE

I have this strong hope that God will continue to use my life as he already has been doing. I've believed for quite a few years that I'm doing exactly what God has called me to do. For whatever reason, he has gifted me to speak to teenagers and share with them truths that help them as they walk in their Christian faith. My hope is that God will allow me to continue to see the fruit of this ministry and that I would be able to continually see students walking with Jesus way beyond high school.

But I also know that in many cases, students that I have worked with have walked away from God. It's in those situations that my hope in God is even stronger because I have to believe and trust that ultimately he will draw them back. I hope that the foundation that they have been given was deep enough and strong enough that ultimately they will be able to work out their faith journey and return to the Lord. For those of you who are walking strong now, my hope and the hope of parents, youth leaders, and your church is that you would continue that journey and allow God to work in your life.

THINK ABOUT:

1. What are some things you hope for in your life?

2. How do you feel knowing that God can renew your hope even when difficult things happen?

3. When do you feel discouraged and without hope? How do you change course in those situations?

THE WORLD THINKS:

Be careful to not hold on to something that isn't real. Hope can be fleeting.

ACT:

Hope is something that can be hard to attain and keep. We have to believe in goodness and truth and believe that God has a plan for us. But when we struggle, those tend to be the things that we let go of first. This is one of those times when you have to stand on the faith of people who are ahead of you on the road of faith. Your "hope" sometimes will be that of others. So find a couple of older Christians in your life and ask them to explain to you how they maintained hope in difficult circumstances.

READ:

Job 5:16, Psalm 25:3, Psalm 33:20, Psalm 62:5, Isaiah 40:31, Acts 24:15, 1 Timothy 4:10, and Hebrews 11:1

FOLLOW-UP

This year is all about you figuring out who you are. In this book, you were first encouraged to define for yourself what you thought about you. Then you were asked to consider what people in your life thought about you—and finally you were given biblical truth to see some of the things God thinks about you.

My prayer (and hope) is that you would somehow reconcile all those things and ultimately see yourself exactly as God sees you. But it's hard and really difficult to do this alone. You will need to stay surrounded by other Christian friends, adults, and a church that can constantly speak truth into your life and help you stay on the path. As I shared earlier, you will face times when you struggle to believe, and during those times you can be reliant on the faith of others to be enough for you as you make sense of it all.